TINTAGEL
OLD POST OFFICE

Cornwall

THE NATIONAL TRUST

A Place of Legends

Big beginnings

Tintagel was a tiny and remote hamlet when this building was first put up in the period between 1350 and 1400. It hugs the ground closely, as it is exposed to the full fury of Atlantic gales. The floor plan suggests that it was a small-scale hall-house, perhaps home to a prosperous yeoman of Trevena, which today is covered by the village of Tintagel. It is a precious survival of such an early domestic dwelling in the south-west corner of England.

A visit from Tennyson

Over the centuries the roof has gradually subsided under the weight of the massive locally quarried slates until it now looks distinctly tipsy. During these centuries it was much altered and extended, and Tintagel has grown around the building,

especially after 1848 when the poet Tennyson spent a wet June day amidst the ruins of Tintagel Castle seeking the spirit of King Arthur. His Arthurian poems made the village famous and much development took place to accommodate the influx of tourists.

The origins of a name

The old hall-house survived, and during the 1870s became the letter-receiving office for the area. It was closed by 1878 after which it became 'The Old Post Office'.

During the 1890s a group of local people, led by Catherine Johns, was concerned that this medieval house might be demolished. They determinedly resolved to rescue it, then had it restored and sold it to the infant National Trust in 1903 for £200.

Strangles Beach looking towards Tintagel

Fore Street, Tintagel, in 1894

Left Painting of the Old Post Office by Reginald Aspinwall, 1885

3

Tour of the House

The Entrance Passage
The house is entered from the street through a porch, on either side of which is a stone bench. The entrance passage, known as an 'entry' in Cornwall, runs through to the garden behind and is comparable to the screens passage in a grander building.

The door to the right leads into the Parlour.

The Parlour
Originally this was probably a service room or an animal shelter, made into a parlour in the 1890s. In the dresser to the right of the hearth are displayed the late eighteenth-century Bossiney Borough tea service, together with the Borough glass, now reduced to a decanter and three wine glasses. Bossiney is a hamlet adjoining Tintagel to the east and had few MPs of eminence – only Sir Francis Drake, who was one of the Borough Members from 1584 to 1586, is remembered today.

Around the room
As well as the Windsor chairs, there is a longcase clock made by Nathaniel Voyce of Mitcheldean in Gloucestershire about 1830, but in an earlier case. The four samplers were all sewn by young girls: Elisabeth Smith, aged 15 in 1837; Frances Rowley (with the Lord's Prayer) in 1768; Eliza Shenton, aged 15, at much the same date; and Mary Ann Thompson, aged 12 (with its delightful house) in 1834.

From the Parlour a narrow steep stair leads up to the North Bedroom.

The Parlour

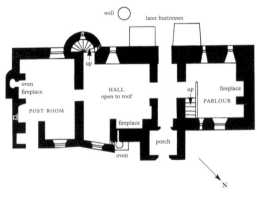

Opposite A narrow slit window in the Parlour, cut from a single piece of greenstone, reveals the great thickness of the walls

The North Bedroom

The room is dominated by its sixteenth-century roof structure, now furnished with a simple iron bedstead and oak and pine furniture. There are four further samplers here, one worked by Caroline Cull, aged 11 in 1832, another by Eliza Hutchins in 1822, one by Eliz Leney dated 1789, and a large alphabet sampler, which is unsigned. Such training exercises were useful for girls going into service who were often required to embroider laundry marks on the domestic linens.

The 'Gallery'

A subsidiary stair, almost a ladder made of slate slabs set into the thickness of the wall, leads to the 'Gallery' overlooking the Hall. This was never a minstrels' gallery of the type found in larger manor houses, but was probably originally a small separate bedchamber lit by the tiny window in the north wall and divided from the Hall by a wall made of timber studding and plaster.

Descending the stairs to the entrance passage, the visitor may step into the garden at the rear of the building.

The Garden

Now on two levels, the garden remains a pleasant spot, despite the very exposed position which the building occupies. The well is conveniently situated close to the back door and is about 10m deep. The semicircular projection towards the east end of this elevation encloses a spiral staircase. The tiny window that lights this staircase is hewn out of a single piece of local greenstone, probably from Polyphant, near Launceston.

Re-entering the building, the visitor turns right into the Hall.

The garden at the back of the house

A needlework sampler, worked by the 11-year-old Caroline Cull in 1832

The North Bedroom

The Hall

This rises the full height of the house to the smoke-blackened rafters. The jambs on either side of the hearth are narrow, high and boldly shaped; they support a large slate overmantel, some eight feet by four feet high (244cm x 122cm). Originally this may have been covered by an elaborate plasterwork panel with either a Biblical scene or a coat of arms. The handsome lacquer cased clock by Oliver Smith of London was made in the mid-eighteenth century. Because of a government tax imposed on private clocks in 1797, these large dial clocks, which were often found in inns or taverns, are frequently known as Act of Parliament clocks.

At the south-west corner of the room a doorway leads to a spiral staircase, and visitors are warned not to bump their heads against the low lintels. The staircase leads into a further bedchamber.

The South Bedroom

Much altered in the 1896 restoration, this bedchamber, possibly with its own latrine in the alcove facing the street, was probably originally approached by a ladder. The oak bed, from a farmhouse on Bodmin Moor, has a feather *tie* (mattress) supported upon ropes threaded in a criss-cross fashion through its frame. The four samplers in this room were worked by Sapience J. Lethbridge, aged 9 in 1833, Elisabeth Palmer, aged 12 in 1813, Temperance Fisher, dated 1834 and donated by a relative in May 2002, and one by Ann Toms, aged 10 which is not dated.

Now descend the stairs and turn right into

Opposite The fireplace in the Hall

The Post Room

This room has been furnished as a Victorian village letter-receiving office, with postal and telegraph equipment located behind the counter. The nearest telegraph office had been at Boscastle, three miles to the north and a busy post throughout the nineteenth century, but by 1890 the telegraph wires had been brought to Tintagel.

An undated needlework sampler by Ann Toms, aged 10

The South Bedroom

A Stormy Past

The post comes to Tintagel

In the early nineteenth century, letters
for Tintagel had to be picked up from
Camelford, five miles away to the south-
west. The increase in postal traffic following
Sir Rowland Hill's introduction of Penny
Postage in 1840 led to the improvement of
postal services in remote country places like
Tintagel. By 1844 the parish was generating
125 letters a week, and so in that year the
General Post Office decided to establish a
letter-receiving office for the district. It
chose Trevena (which was the pre-Victorian
name of the village) as the most central of
the several scattered villages and hamlets
comprising the large parish of Tintagel.

Tintagel under threat

In the late nineteenth century, tourism
reached Tintagel. Visitors were drawn
not only by the spectacular coastal scenery
around Barras Nose, but also by the
romance of Tintagel's legendary past.
Tennyson's *Idylls of the King* made Tintagel
famous as the birthplace of King Arthur.
Barras Nose was bought in 1897 by local
subscribers and became the first coastal
property acquired by the National Trust in
England.

The result of this popularity can
be seen in the village of Tintagel and its
surroundings today. Many old cottages
were torn down and replaced by guest-
houses, shops and hotels, the largest of
which, The Camelot Castle Hotel, still
stands at the bottom of the village street
on the edge of the cliffs.

Few of the picturesque buildings of
the old village survived this onslaught,
and in 1892 the owner of the Old Post Office
decided to sell it for redevelopment and
gave notice to the GPO, which moved its
business across the street. By 1895 the
building had become virtually derelict
and was put up for auction.

Spagnoletti Telegraph
Undulator Receiver –
used to receive and send
telegraph messages in
Victorian England

A novelty postcard
from 1914

View of Barras Nose

The Post comes to Tintagel

The Building

The Old Post Office is built of the local brown slate (long since weathered to an even grey) and the occasional piece of granite. Granite was also used for the heavy arch over the entrance doorway and local greenstone for the window surrounds. The walls are between 75 and 100cm thick, but despite their massive construction, they have had to be buttressed at the back to support the immense weight of the stone roof slates, which came from nearby Cliff Quarry. The stout chimneystacks, the main one in three stages, are provided with slate drips and stepped slate flashings, and are capped with the local pattern of chimneypot consisting of four slates set on edge. These features were once common in north Cornwall, but are fast disappearing.

The plan is typical of many late medieval hall-houses, with a central single-storey hall open to the roof, flanked by smaller service rooms and a kitchen (now the Parlour), with bedrooms above. In spite of its small scale, the house is surprisingly spacious.

Recent discoveries

A historical survey carried out in 2003 greatly increased our knowledge of how the Old Post Office has changed over the years. Originally built as a three-room hall-house in the later fourteenth century, in the sixteenth century the thatched roof was replaced by slate, and the hall fireplace added a little later, followed by an extension in the same room to provide a bay on to the roadside. Perhaps at the same time the first floors were inserted and the South Bedroom made larger. Fireplaces were introduced later, as were some of the characterful

mullion and greenstone windows, which may have come from other, now demolished, buildings.

Furniture

The building came to the National Trust empty of contents, apart from the hall table, and since then the rooms have been furnished with things from farmhouses and cottages in the vicinity. The furniture is nearly all of oak, which until recently was commonly found in this part of Cornwall.

Displays

A small collection of needlework samplers is being assembled in some of the rooms. These small embroidered panels, the earliest here dating from the mid-eighteenth century, were usually worked by girls in coloured silks on a linen ground, and incorporate stylised birds and flowers, the letters of the alphabet and short moral or religious texts. They were usually signed and dated by the embroiderer.

The local slate roof and the chimney stack from the front

Hydrangeas in the front garden

The rear wall is heavily buttressed to support the immense weight of the local slate roof

A Street in Tintagel

A postcard of Fore Street, Tintagel, in the late 19th century

Saving the Old Post Office

A group of local artists, who had loved the village as it was, became concerned at the threat of redevelopment to the Old Post Office. One of them, Catherine Johns, decided to act. 'Of a most hospitable and large-hearted nature,' according to her obituary, 'she was never so content as when entertaining her numerous friends and neighbours.' She bought the building for £350 on the understanding that means would be found to preserve it. Sales of prints after pictures by several well-known artists were held in 1896 to raise money. Shortly afterwards the fabric of the building was carefully repaired by the leading Arts and Crafts architect Detmar Blow according to the strict principles laid down by the Society for the Protection of Ancient Buildings.

In 1900 the National Trust agreed to buy the building from Catherine Johns for a nominal £200, which was raised by public appeal. The purchase was subject to a lease to Miss Johns for her lifetime and the building was finally vested in the Trust in 1903.

Roof restoration

After almost another century of Cornish gales, the Old Post Office again required attention. In 1992 it was discovered that many of the beams under the ancient roof were rotten and needed replacement. A local firm of builders took off the original slates, renewed or repaired the affected beams and then replaced them. The roof now looks much as it did before, with the many undulations carefully retained. The cost of the work was partially met by generous grants from English Heritage and Delabole Slate, formally a division of RTZ Mining and Exploration Ltd.

A sketch made by Detmar Blow for his restoration of the Old Post Office in 1896

Below The roof under repair in 1992

Opposite Fore Street around 1900, when much of the village had already been rebuilt to accommodate visitors

The Old Post Office, in
Dinah Maria Craik's *An
Unsentimental Journey
through Cornwall* (1884)